Voices in the Shadows

poems written by youth at Echo Glen Children's Center

Kiana Davis

editor

Tree Root Strong Publishing, LLC 2018

ISBN 978-0-9907548-2-4

Book Cover Designer Kiana Davis

Images taken from Storyblocks.com

Blank Journal Background
Pencil: Pencil
Youth walking into the light

Publisher and Book Designer: Kiana Davis

Tree Root Strong Publishing, LLC
www. PoeticAwakenings.com

Dedication

This book is dedicated to the awesome youth at the Echo Glen Children's Center for writing with me and opening their hearts to the art of poetry.

Table of Contents

Chapter 4 Wishes

Chapter 5 Changes

Chapter 6 Strength

Acknowledgements

The Poetry in the Shadows Project was inspired by resilient and creative youth at the Echo Glen Children's Facility. I would like to thank all the youth at Echo Glen who wrote and shared pieces of their souls on paper. And thank you to all the amazing staff who support and serve the youth each day.

Thank you so much, 4Culture, for awarding me the Arts Grant and believing in the Voices in the Shadows project.

Thank you, Carmen Rivera for inviting me to teach poetry workshops at Echo Glen and encouraging the students to write and share their hearts. Thank you for joining in on many of the sessions and writing and sharing your poems with the students.

Thank you, Richard Gold for your amazing free poetry templates on www.PongoTeenWriting.com. Your templates and poetry writing methods are so awesome! Students wrote poems using templates: I Wish, 10 Reasons to Love Me, Wish Poem #1, and Strength.

Thank you Jelia Farr and Jennifer Wooten for helping me format and edit the book.

This project was supported, in part, by an award from 4Culture.

Chapter 1

Poetry Is

Poetry is a Way of Life
Luis (13)

Poetry is a way of life.
It sounds like rhythm and melody.
It gives passion and knowledge.
Poetry looks like a lifestyle.
It knows all things and nothing.
It hears rhythm.
It teaches me how to feel and love.
Poetry is everything in life for me.
I have always gone to poetry for everything.

Poetry is Our Soul in Voice
Katie W. (15)

Poetry is our soul in voice
It sounds like sincerity and meaningfulness
It gives heart, feelings and passion.
Poetry looks like words from the heart
It knows everything especially dreams
It hears people's thoughts and dreams
It teaches perspective.
Poetry is voice.

Poetry is Expressing Yourself to Fullest
Boo M. (15)

Poetry is expressing yourself to fullest
It sounds like the tiny noises of the world around us
It gives emotions to everything

Poetry looks like a shade of color that has no name
It knows how to speak to the soul of everyone
It hears the voice inside of everyone
It teaches how often people see the world
Poetry is looking at the world through other people.

Poetry is an Emotion
Silvia L. (17)

Poetry is an emotion people seek
to express through people
It sounds like ocean waves crashing through the share waiting
to free themselves
It gives blissful meaning to your expression
Poetry looks like the promise of hope
It knows no meaning of good or bad
It hears the despair of people waiting
to get something off their chest.
It teaches me you how to free yourself
Poetry is change

Poetry is a Wolf Song
Erin S. (15)

Poetry is like a song.
It sounds like the sound of an Ocarina.
It gives a purpose of what they want others to see.
Poetry looks like a wolf.
It knows how you are feeling.
It hears your heartbeat and your sadness.
It teaches others to understand.
Poetry is a wolf song.

Poetry is Our Stories
Trisa S. (15)

Poetry is a way to accept the hardships that you go through
It sounds like a voice within us that has some trouble
being heard.
It gives meaning to the words that not everyone listens to.
Poetry looks like cursive on pink paper
It knows what we mean even if it doesn't make sense
It hears our words that we need to get out,
when we don't have the confidence to say them.
It teaches us how to make ourselves be heard.
Poetry is our stories.

Poetry is Something You Write
Rocio R. (17)

Poetry is something you write.
It is what your heart is feeling.
It sounds like when a heart crying or laughing.
It gives emotion
Poetry looks like words flying through the air.
It knows what it is feeling.
It hears your weeping and gratitude
It teaches life lessons.
Poetry is what your heart desires to let go.
When you fall in love
When the storms are strong
how at midnight the moon shines
through your brown glowing skin,
He kisses you gently, softly everlasting lips,
while you fall in love all over again.

Poetry is the Soul
Diamond T. (17)

    Poetry is soul
    It sounds like the wind
    It gives you hope for tomorrow
    because it will show you the way
    Poetry looks like the night sky.
    It knows that you're looking to the sky
    It hears your wishes
    It teaches you hope
    Poetry is life

Poetry is the Way Outta Panic
Martha S. (18)

Poetry is the way outta panic
It sounds like a rip in universe's fabric
It gives me a reason to breathe
Poetry looks like broken children with hopeful dreams.
It knows who you are
It hears you when you rip open your deepest scars.
I wrote poetry as an escape to stop self-harm.
Poetry is who I am.

Poetry is Expressing Your Feelings
Alicia S. (17)

Poetry is expressing your feelings.
It sounds like going through your mind
It gives hope and faith
Because you need hope and faith
in order to survive.
Poetry looks like the unknown
It knows about you
It hears your feelings
It teaches you what you are thinking or feeling
Poetry is expressing your feelings.

Poetry is an Amazing Way to Live
Bill L. (13)

> Poetry is a song that does not have to rhyme.
> It sounds like a small hint of life
> or a hummingbird humming.
> It gives a way of life.
> Poetry look like a small living animal or hummingbird.
> It knows that anyone can understand it.
> It hears a whistle or hum in the air.
> It teaches a way of life.
> Poetry is an amazing way to live.

Poetry is an Alternative Reality
Patrick B. (14)

Poetry is an alternative reality
because it's a place to escape away from the pain.
It sounds like calm sweet song.
It gives emotional entertainment
Poetry looks like moving words on paper.
It hears my emotions and thoughts
It teaches me the ways of life.
Poetry is life.

Poetry is a Way of Life
Fisher A. (16)

Poetry is a way of life
Without it I would be lost.
It sounds like a story from someone's soul.
It gives you more purpose in life.
Poetry looks like a 300-page book
It knows everything and anything
It hears ourselves in our own true place
It bears common knowledge people fail to see
Poetry is more than what people make it to be
If you try it, it could set you free.

Poetry is too Emotional
Allie T. (14)

      Poetry is too emotional
      It sounds like depressing songs
      It gives people back their experiences
      Poetry looks like beautiful sadness
      It knows everything
      It hears everything
      It teaches how to connect with your past emotions.
      Poetry is life all over again.

22

Chapter 2

Walls

White Walls
Hunter L. (16)

I sit in my cell
pondering my own existence
wondering if you're worth all my resistance
and I try too hard to make sure that you like me
and I think too much about the past that we had
because I'm sitting here on a summer day
Staring at white walls
Tallying the years away
and I know it's all my fault
I'm sitting here on a summer day
and I forgot what the moon looks like
but I know in time that I'll find what I'm looking for
but for now, I'm fine
I know I'm not but that's ok
I sit in my cell
pondering my own existence
wondering if you're worth all my resistance
and I think it's time to realize that petty crime doesn't mean a
thing.
and I think I'll try to turn my life back over again
because I'm sitting here on a summer day
staring at white walls
tallying the years away
wondering when I'll be free again.

Four Walls
Jubal H. (16)

Four walls all white
Locked doors
no one in sight
Take a trip with me
Into my day dream
Everyone is welcome to learn the unseen
No money to get in
Sit on the side lines
Try to listen in
Try and escape
from the emotions that I feel
No fantasy
wait to keep the emotions sealed.

She Hides
Allie T. (14)

> She hides away behind a door
> She kept locked
> But the walls weren't' thick enough
> To block out angry noises of the voices
> That once soothed her to sleep.
>
> Every night I go to bed praying
> For the promise of tomorrow in my head.
> I fall in love with the stars,
> I miss the sound of the cars,
> When I get out
> I will be roaming all about
> And instead of getting locked away.
> I will be able to pray for the promise of the next day.

Music Helps my Pain
Marta M. (15)

      Music helps my pain
      Eases my gain
      I feel hopeless at times
      So I listen to music that rhymes
      From a tough neighborhood,
      Beneath all the wood,
      I am not alone
      It helped me find my throne
      I identify myself
      Music can help.

Music is the Change
Audree L. (16)

Music is the change in you
Music is the sway and jump in my step
Music is where you go to when there is nothing else
Music is how the world should be
Music is what makes you want to move
Music is who you want to be.

Music is my Escape
Tyra B.

    Music is my mother's voice.
    Music is the key to the streets.
    Music is loud.
    Music is the key to success.
    Music is soul.
    Music is my escape.

Chapter 3

Sometimes

Poems inspired by Tupac Shakur's Poem: I Cry

Sometimes I will Never Understand Why
Hunter L. (16)

Sometimes I sleep and I don't know why
Sometimes I cry because I feel they don't know why
Sometimes I wish I could fly just so they don't know why
Sometimes I will never understand why
Sometimes I cry because my heart is torn
Because I no longer have you to keep me warm
Sometimes I feel I need to confine my emotions
Sometimes I will never understand
those confined emotions
Sometimes I will never understand why.

Sometimes I Ask Myself Why
Chad D. (15)

    Sometimes I think of things that have happened in my life
    I feel like things never really go right
    I ask myself why I did the things i did….
    But i don't have an answer
    and I don't know why
    The world moves fast, and it would rather pass you by
    Than stop and see what makes you cry
    People say it's not manly to cry
    I never had the nerve to ask them why.

Sometimes I Feel Like Things Will Never Get Better
Levon

Sometimes I feel like things will never get better.
That doors of opportunity will never open.
That I'll always deal with problems alone
Because the world moves fast and would rather pass you by
Nobody really cares so why cry
I'll just keep it pushin and never ask why
My life is so hard.

Sometimes I Stare up at The Sky
Sam (16)

> Sometimes I stare up at the sky
> And wonder why this life turns out this way
> We fight
> We live
> We love
> We die
> And hardly anyone asks why
> Why are we here
> And what do we leave behind
> Our imaginations
> They flow with life brimming from the start
> but they take no form
> the form we give them, meaningless.

Sometimes I Hear People Laughing
Roger G. (15)

Sometimes I hear people laughing
and I wonder why they are happy
when I am not.

Sometimes I think I Should do Right
Matt M. (16)

Sometimes I think I should do right
But I don't
and sometimes it makes me cry
Sometimes I do wrong
And it makes me feel strong.

Sometimes I am Scared Because I'm worried
Bobby (16)

Sometimes I don't know
but it's worse when I do know
but can't do anything about it

Sometimes I am scared because I'm worried
about my family and friends
because I know the struggle they go through

sometimes I cry among my friends
but they are more like brothers
because of what we've been through together.

You helped me through
What I could never have gone through alone

You reached inside my head
and pulled brilliance
out of madness

You heard me
Before I could even say
All the things i needed to tell you.

But now you're gone
Now it's' too late
Now, I sit here wondering
If I'll ever see you again.

Now the only great thing I can do
Is lie low
Keep quiet
Act as though nothing is wrong.
When in reality
Everything I know is falling apart
And soon.

There'll be nothing left

Chapter 4

Wishes

.

I Wish
Matt M.
Dedicated to my dad

When I was young I used to wish to travel into time
Today I wish I could change what I've done
Every day I wish I hadn't done what I've done
My wish is the color of a dark red flame
and it burns inside of me.
It is the sound of crickets chirping
just waiting for me to explode
My wish feels like bomb just ticking away.
My wish is always with me
My wish is never going to leave
My wish is always going to stay with me.

Second Chances
Sam (16)

We met one day
Long ago
And at the end of it
I wished it would never end.
But it did
Like all things
Come to an end.
But unlike all things
He came back
A few years later
Giving me
A second chance,
To get it right.
But I failed
Everyday
I sit and think
Replaying words in my head
If only
If I hadn't done what I done
If I hadn't
If I hadn't

Wishes
Bobby (16)

When I was young I used to wish I could fly
Today I wish I could keep my feet on the ground
Every day I wish I could get just ten more
dollars in my pocket
My wish is the color of a black flag
hanging out my right pocket
It is the sound of a lighter sparking in the distance
My wish feels like saying just once knowing
you are going to do it again.

My wish will always be fantasy
My wish is never realistic
My wish is not a possibility.

Friends
Levon

When I was young I used to wish to have friends
that would accept me for who I am.
Today I wish I could have told him how much he helped me
cope with people.
Every day I wish I could see him again
That he'll come back
My wish is the color of the biggest rain cloud
there has ever been
It is the sound of a thousand cries
My wish feels like it'll never come true
My wish is always going to be the same forever
My wish is never going to change not one bit
My wish is hopeful but not expected to come true.

Freedom
Chad D. (15)

When I was young I used to wish for fortune and fame
Today I wish for freedom I can claim
Every day I wish to show I'm not the same
My wish is the color red autumn leaves falling from the trees.
It is the sound of a crackling fire
My wish feels like a crisp winter breeze

My wish is always exceeding
My wish is never fleeting
My wish is what makes me.

Reality
Roger G. (15)

When I was young I used to wish
that I could play outside all day
Today I wish that I had kept wishing that
Every day I wish that I had made
better choices instead of trying to be hard
My wish is the color of a blue flag now
but I wish it wasn't.
It is the sound of shots ringing out at night.
My wish feels like forever 'till eternity

My wish is always the same.
My wish is never appreciated.
My wish is not a reality.

Free
Gibson B. (15)

When I was young I used to wish
to go outside in the sun and have fun.
Today I wish to be free and live
life to the fullest and to not be foolish
Every day I wish to fly
My wish is the color of the sky
Baby blue is true
baby blue is the sky
baby blue don't lie.

Untitled
Raymond

Except
I hope I don't ever end up back in this hole
I lived by the rules, so I'm never told.
I may not be perfect, but I can understand.
I always wish for my family.
I do my best to understand what the purpose is.
I can create happiness.
I want the people around me to feel happy.
I hold onto some things forever, my experiences
I have unusual ideas like how to fix things.
If I were an animal, I'd be my spirit animal (wolf).
I have secret talent- I can always smile.

End
Genesis (17)

I hope that racism will have an end
But when
Will it ever have and end?

It's like an unfinished story
We still wonder and hope

When will racism have an end?

Chapter 5

Changes

Choices
Katie W. (15)

Don't take what you want
But take what you need
You can put that together
And call that success
You can lose those fears

All those bad years
You can put all these bad memories
And most of those tears

You can flush them down that drain
And not let them become life's pain
or you can let them get to. you
And believe like all the same

I finally got out of treatment and was a new me
Really thought I had the key to be free
But all of a sudden they just wanted me to leave
And I couldn't believe
They pushed me down
I got up and wiped the dirt off my sleeve
Then went back to the streets
Sent back to the part of me none of my family should see
And I really realized my heart
That the more that I go the more that it bleeds

The more that I stay.
The more they want me to leave
And don't want to live
So I sit and believe

All this pain that is caused is all because of me.

I dream about the nights
I was happy with the fallen
Knowing they're just memories of happiness
Again without the feelings of emptiness
Without the feelings of emptiness
Agony in my soul.
Because I wasn't there when they needed me
I was running in the street when I shouldn't have been
They cried for my help and I couldn't see
I was on my way to wealth
Just to try to pay the fee
And I really felt that drugs were key
I didn't know I was on the edge to lose what I needed
And I really messed up because they want to see me leave
Then I thought to myself "How could it be?"
Then I looked back to see myself gone by the week
When they were down on their knees
Praying for the pain to get up and leave
And I was coming home with lies through my teeth
Running from the cops
Doing things they didn't want to believe.

I think of those sleepless nights
With their death on mind
Trying not to think
That I lost all my shine

Replacing that faith
With the hustle and grind
Making up that happiness
With all the happiness set aside.

Wisdom
Boo M. (14)

See the wisdom
Without myths
Affecting your choices
Face your fear

Don't search
For hideaways
Call for help
It'll lead you to success
And radiance commits to
Realistic promises.

I Would Change
by Allie T. (14)

I would change people.
I love my sisters
I would change the way everything affects us.
I love my sisters.
I would change my emotions.
I would change their life.

Voice in the Wind
Fisher A. (16)

I feel lost like a voice in the wind
Being pushed around
A leaf lost in a sea of water struggling to reach dry land
I feel lost like a voice in the wind
Trying to make my family proud
Screwing up like an error in math
I feel like a voice in the wind
Shouting out asking for help
But only wishing I could change
My own on and off depression.

Erase
Trisa S. (15)

      I would change the bad in my life.
      Change all the wrong that I've done back to right.
      I would bring up my grades and change my last name
      And if I had a choice
      I would erase unwanted fame.

Newborn
Alicia S. (17)

I would like to change my age
I would like to change to be a better mom
I would like to change my way for my boyfriend
I would like to change for the better
To back to when I was a newborn
To would go back to being a virgin
To would go back to not using drugs.

In a World Where Everything is Invisible
by Jubal H. (17)

In a world where everything is invisible
people think my goals are inconceivable
In a world where everything is so fragile
in the last dying breath all we need is revival

you need people
from the broken
and the ghetto
to come up and change the world
for the better.

Chapter 6

Strength

.

You Helped me
Sam (16)

You helped me through
What I could never have gone through alone.
You reached inside my head
And pulled brilliance
Out of madness

You heard me
Before I could even say
All things I needed to tell you.

But now you're gone
Now it's too late
Now, I sit here wondering
If I'll ever see you again.

Now the only great thing I can do
Is lie low,
Keep quiet
Act as though nothing's wrong
When in reality
Everything I know is falling apart soon.

There'll be nothing left.

I Can
Davidson B. (12)

I can be as strong as a bear
Ready to strike

I can be as strong as the sea
Pay attention to my swirling waves
I will strike anyone who comes too close.

I can be as strong in ways you don't expect
I can be as strong as a palm tree
Able to protect you from the burning sun.

My strength can be gentle
I can be as strong as a friend
Ready to put you on my back.

Strong
by Alex C. (16)

I can be as strong as a savage
Ready to jump at any moment
I can be as strong as the strong winds blowing
Pay attention to my howling growl
I will blow away anyone who comes my way.

Strength
Armando K. (16)

>I can be strong as a wall
>Ready to brace myself
>I can be as strong as the tree
>Pay attention to my leaves
>I will blow you away with beauty
>
>I can be strong in ways you don't expect
>I can be strong as a memory
>Able to bring back thoughts of glory.
>
>My strength can be gentle.
>It can be strong as a rock
>Ready to stand up for myself.

Strong
Fisher A. (16)

I can be as strong as a Locker
Ready to protect my secrets

I can be as strong as the atom bomb
Pay attention to my mushroom cloud
I will poison those who come too close

I can be strong in ways you don't expect.
I ca be as strong as a Dragon
Able to Burn you up.

My strength can be gentle
I ca be as strong as a Emu
Ready lay to a big egg.

I can be strong and change the world.
I can be as forgiving as the future.
I can show you who I am.

Stuck
Levon

400 and something nights locked in the cell
Stuck thinking
Reminiscing about the past
days and months to go before
they open the gates to freedom
I wonder about things on the other side

10 Ten Reasons to Love Me
Allie T. (14)

I may not be perfect, but I can keep a smile on my face.
I always wish for others to be happy.
I do my best to understand how people
can be so disrespectful.
I can create my own world.
I want the people around me to feel great about themselves
and everyone around them.
I hold onto some things forever, like a great memory.
I have unusual ideas, like fun things to fill my time with.
If I were an animal, I'd be a puppy.
I have a secret talent- I can sing.
I am beautiful.

10 Ten Reasons to Love Me
Marta M. (15)

I may not be perfect, but I can love past my pain.
I always wish for someone who can show me new things
I do my best to understand why you
treated me the way you did.
I can create imaginary memories that make me feel safe.
I want the people around me to feel
my pain but learn from it.
I hold onto some things forever, like the love
I used to have for you.
I have unusual ideas, like doing crazy things to get you back.
If I were an animal, I'd be a unicorn.
I have a secret talent- I can forgive things
and people that tried to kill me.
I am alone and fighting for my throne.

Beauty
Marta M. (15)

Beauty is all she knows
She covers up her woes.
She cries at night
Even though she claims she all right.
She tries to put up a fight
But she never wins at the end of the night.

Black Man
Tyra B. (18)

>Strong black man
>Man, is he in pain
>That black man
>He is a slave
>That black man
>He is just in a struggle

See the Wisdom
Boo M. (14)

See the wisdom without myths
Affecting your choices.
Face your fear
Don't' search for hideaways
Call for help
It'll led you to success and radiance
Commit to realized promises.

www.ingramcontent.com/pod-product-compliance
Lightning Source LLC
Chambersburg PA
CBHW071634040426
42452CB00009B/1624